How To Use Tiktok To Grow Your Business And Personal Brand:

Beginner's Guide

Fidelis Okoh

DEDICATION

This book is dedicated to "YOU" reading this book and anyone hustling to make it online. You can achieve your goals only if you take action, and reading this book is a big step forward. Congratulations!

TABLE OF CONTENTS

CHAPTER ONE: INTRODUCTION

TikTok has taken the social media world by storm, quickly becoming one of the most popular and influential platforms with over 1 billion active users worldwide. This explosive growth has created a unique opportunity for businesses and individuals to build their brands and reach new audiences.

In this e-book, we'll explore how to use TikTok to grow your business or personal brand. We'll dive into the importance of using TikTok, the benefits it offers, and why it's become such an essential tool for branding and marketing.

We'll cover everything from understanding the TikTok platform, its algorithm, and its user base to identifying your target audience and creating compelling content. We'll also explore strategies for building and growing your following, monetizing your TikTok presence, and best practices for success.

Whether you're a business owner or an individual looking to build your personal brand, this e-book will provide you with valuable insights and practical strategies for using TikTok effectively. Let's get started and unlock the full potential of TikTok for your brand.

CHAPTER 2: UNDERSTANDING TIKTOK

TikTok is a social media platform that allows users to create and share short videos, usually set to music. It was launched in China in 2016 under the name Douyin and was later released globally as TikTok in 2018. Since then, it has rapidly grown in popularity, with over 1 billion active users worldwide, making it one of the most popular social media apps available today.

In this chapter, we will explore the key features and functions of TikTok, the platform's user base, the TikTok algorithm, and common misconceptions about the app

1. Overview of TikTok Platform and its User Base

TikTok's user base is predominantly made up of Gen Z and

millennials, with the majority of users aged between 16 and 24 years old. The app has a predominantly female audience, with around 60% of users being female. However, baby boomers and big brands are becoming increasingly attracted to the high customer traffic it offers. TikTok is available in over 150 markets and in 75 languages, making it a truly global platform. It is an app that allows users to create and share short videos, usually set to music.

2. Key Features and Functions of the App

TikTok's main feature is the short-form video content, which can be up to 60 seconds long. Users can create videos by selecting music and using special effects, filters, and editing tools. Additionally, users can follow other users, like and comment on videos, and share videos with friends and followers. TikTok also has a "For You" page, which is a personalized feed of videos that are recommended to users based on their activity on the app.

3. How TikTok Algorithm Works

TikTok's algorithm uses machine learning to show users the content they are most likely to engage with based on their activity on the app. The algorithm considers a range of factors, such as watch time, likes, comments, shares, and more. It also takes into account the user's previous activity and preferences to provide personalized content recommendations. The algorithm constantly evolves and updates to ensure that users are seeing the most relevant and engaging content possible.

4. Common Misconceptions about TikTok

One of the most common misconceptions about TikTok is that it's only for teenagers and young adults. However, TikTok's user base is becoming increasingly diverse, and there are many opportunities for businesses and individuals to reach new audiences. Another misconception is that TikTok is all about lip-syncing and dancing videos. While these types of videos are popular, there are many other types of content, including cooking, travel, and educational content, that perform well on the platform.

It is also important to note that TikTok can be a powerful tool for businesses and individuals to promote their products or services.

In conclusion, understanding the basics of TikTok is crucial for anyone looking to leverage the platform for personal branding or business marketing. With its unique features and rapidly growing user base, TikTok presents exciting opportunities for users to reach and engage with a wide audience.

In the following chapters, we will dive deeper into how to use TikTok to grow your brand effectively.

CHAPTER 3: IDENTIFYING YOUR BRAND AND AUDIENCE

In this chapter, we will discuss the importance of developing a strong brand identity and identifying your target audience on TikTok. Additionally, we will provide tips on how to create content that resonates with your audience and how to research your competition on the platform.

1. Developing a Strong Brand Identity for TikTok

Your brand identity is what sets you apart from the competition and helps you connect with your target audience. When it comes to TikTok, it's essential to develop a brand identity that aligns with the platform's values and culture. TikTok is all about creativity, authenticity, and relatability. As such, your brand should reflect those values. To create a strong brand identity on TikTok, start by defining your brand's mission, values, and personality. What sets your brand apart? What are your core values? What type of personality do you want to convey to your audience? Once you have a clear understanding of your brand identity, you can start creating content that aligns with those values.

2. Identifying Your Target Audience on the Platform

Understanding your target audience is key to creating content that resonates with them. On TikTok, the user base is primarily made up of Gen Z and millennials. However, it's essential to go beyond age and consider other factors such as interests, values, and demographics. To identify your target audience on TikTok, start by researching popular trends, hashtags, and challenges on the platform. Look at the content your competitors are creating and the type of engagement they are getting. This information can help you get a better understanding of the type of content that resonates with your target audience.

3. Understanding What Types of Content Perform Well on TikTok

TikTok is all about short-form, engaging, and entertaining videos. The platform's algorithm prioritizes content that is engaging and keeps users on the app for longer. As such, it's essential to create content that is both entertaining and informative. Some types of content that perform well on TikTok include:

Challenges and trends: Participating in popular challenges and trends can help you increase your visibility on the platform and reach a wider audience.

Educational content: TikTok users love learning new things, and educational content that is easy to digest performs well on the platform.

Behind-the-scenes content: Giving your audience a glimpse behind the scenes of your brand can help build trust and foster a deeper connection with your audience.

4. How to Research Your Competition on TikTok

Researching your competition on TikTok is crucial to stay on top of industry trends and ensuring your content is staying relevant. Start by identifying your top competitors on the platform and analyzing their content. Look at the type of content they are creating, the engagement they are getting, and the hashtags they are using. Additionally, keep an eye on popular trends and challenges in your industry and see how your competitors are participating. This information can help you create content that is more engaging and relevant to your target audience.

CHAPTER 4: CREATING COMPELLING CONTENT

TikTok is all about engaging and entertaining content that keeps viewers hooked. As you develop your presence on the platform, it's important to create content that not only captures your brand's essence but also resonates with your target audience.

In this chapter, we'll explore tips and tricks to help you create compelling content that stands out on TikTok.

1. Tips for creating engaging and shareable content

The first step in creating great TikTok content is to understand what works well on the platform. Here are some tips to help you create engaging and shareable content:

Keep it short and sweet: TikTok videos are typically around 15 seconds long, so make sure your content is concise and to the point.

Use eye-catching visuals: Bright colors, interesting camera angles, and unique props can help your videos stand out in a sea of content.

Add music and sound effects: TikTok's music library is vast and can help set the tone for your video. Additionally, incorporating sound effects can add humour and enhance the overall viewing experience.

Utilize text overlays: Adding text overlays to your videos can help convey a message or highlight important information.

2. Understanding TikTok's video format and creative tools

TikTok's video format is unique in that it's vertical and takes up the entire screen. As such, it's important to use the platform's creative tools to their full potential. Here are some of the features you can use to enhance your videos:

Filters and effects: TikTok offers a wide range of filters and effects to enhance your videos. From face filters to animations, there's something for everyone.

Stickers and emojis: Adding stickers and emojis to your videos can help convey emotions and add humor.

Text and captions: As mentioned earlier, text overlays can be a powerful tool to convey a message or highlight important information.

Duet feature: The duet feature allows users to collaborate with other users by creating a split-screen video.

3. **How to incorporate storytelling and humour into your content**

One of the best ways to create engaging content is by telling a story or using humour. Here are some tips to help you incorporate these elements into your TikTok content:

Keep it relatable: Stories that viewers can relate to tend to perform well on TikTok.

Use humour: Humour is a universal language that can help your content appeal to a wider audience.

Use a hook: Starting your video with a hook can help grab viewers' attention and keep them engaged throughout the video.

4. Utilizing Trends and Challenges on Tiktok

Finally, one of the easiest ways to create engaging content is by participating in TikTok trends and challenges. These are popular themes or hashtags that many users are using in their videos. By jumping on board with a trend or challenge, you can increase the visibility of your content and connect with a wider audience.

In conclusion, creating compelling content on TikTok requires a combination of creativity, storytelling, and a good understanding of the platform's unique features. By following the tips and tricks outlined in this chapter, you'll be well on your way to creating TikTok content that resonates with your target audience and grows your brand or personal presence on the platform.

CHAPTER 5: BUILDING AND GROWING YOUR FOLLOWING

One of the primary goals of using TikTok for your business or personal brand is to reach a wider audience and grow your following. In this chapter, we will explore various strategies to help you achieve this goal:

1. Strategies for Increasing Your Tiktok Following

When you first start using TikTok, building a following can be a challenge. However, there are several strategies you can use to increase your following on the platform, such as:

Consistency: Posting consistently is key to building your following on TikTok. Try to post at least once a day to keep your audience engaged and interested in your content.

Engage with other users: Interact with other users by commenting, liking, and sharing their content. This will help you build relationships with other TikTok users and potentially attract new followers to your account.

Cross-promotion: Promote your TikTok account on your other social media platforms and vice versa. This will help you reach a wider audience and attract new followers to your TikTok account.

3. Using Hashtags and TikTok Trends to Increase Visibility

Hashtags are an essential part of TikTok, and using the right ones can help increase the visibility of your content. When selecting hashtags, consider the following:

Relevance: Use hashtags that are relevant to your content and target audience.

Popularity: Use popular hashtags that are frequently searched for on the platform to increase the visibility of your content.

Trending hashtags: Keep an eye on trending hashtags and participate in challenges and trends to increase your visibility and reach.

4. How to Collaborate with Other TikTok Users to Grow Your Following

Collaborating with other TikTok users can be an effective way to increase your following on the platform. Some ways to collaborate with other users include:

Duets: Create a duet with another user's video to showcase your creativity and potentially attract their followers to your account.

Challenges: Participate in challenges with other users and collaborate on creating content that showcases both of your brands.

Cross-promotion: Partner with another TikTok user to cross-promote each other's content and reach a wider audience.

4 Tips for Engaging with Your TikTok Audience

Engaging with your audience is crucial to building a loyal following on TikTok. Some tips for engaging with your audience include:

Responding to comments: Responding to comments on your videos is a great way to build relationships with your audience and show them that you value their input.

Hosting Q&A sessions: Hosting Q&A sessions are a fun way to interact with your audience and provide them with valuable information about your brand.

Creating user-generated content: Encourage your audience to create content related to your brand, and share and engage with their content on your account.

By using these strategies, you can effectively build and grow your following on TikTok, increasing your reach and potential for success

CHAPTER 6: MONETIZING YOUR TIKTOK PRESENCE

TikTok has quickly become a popular social media platform, and its user base continues to grow every day. With such a large audience, it's no surprise that TikTok has also become a popular platform for creators to monetize their presence.

In this chapter, we'll explore some of the ways you can monetize your TikTok presence, whether you're looking to grow your business or personal brand.

1. Overview of TikTok's monetization options

TikTok offers several ways for creators to monetize their content. Here are some of the most popular options:

In-app purchases: TikTok offers virtual coins that users can purchase and use to buy virtual gifts for their favourite creators. Creators can then exchange these gifts for real money.

Brand partnerships: Brands are always on the lookout for creators with a large following on TikTok. By partnering with brands, creators can earn money through sponsored posts, product reviews, and other types of branded content.

Live streaming: TikTok offers a live streaming feature that allows creators to interact with their audience in real time. Viewers can purchase virtual gifts during these live streams, which creators can exchange for real money.

Creator Fund: TikTok has created a Creator Fund that pays eligible creators for their content. To be eligible for the Creator Fund, creators must meet certain criteria, such as having at least 100,000 followers and meeting a specific engagement rate.

2. Partner with brands on TikTok

Partnering with brands on TikTok can be a lucrative way to monetize your presence. Here are some tips on how to find brand partnerships on TikTok:

Build a strong following: Brands are more likely to partner with creators who have a large following on TikTok. Focus on creating engaging content that resonates with your audience and helps you grow your following.

Reach out to brands: Don't be afraid to reach out to brands that align with your niche. You can start by sending them a direct message on TikTok, but it's also a good idea to research their contact information and reach out to them via email.

Be authentic: Brands want to work with creators who align with their values and mission. Make sure you're only partnering with brands that align with your own values, and that you're creating authentic content that resonates with your audience.

3. **Monetize your TikTok account through product sales or affiliate marketing**

If you have a product or service to sell, TikTok can be a powerful tool for driving sales. Here are some tips on how to monetize your TikTok account through product sales or affiliate marketing:

Create engaging content: Make sure you're creating engaging content that showcases your product or service in a way that resonates with your audience. You can create product demos, how-to videos, or other types of content that show off your product's features.

Use affiliate marketing: Affiliate marketing is a great way to earn money by promoting products or services that align with your niche. You can sign up for affiliate programs through companies like Amazon or Rakuten, and then promote their products on your TikTok account.

Offer exclusive discounts: Consider offering exclusive discounts to your TikTok followers to incentivize them to make a purchase. You can create unique discount codes that can only be used on your website or offer limited-time discounts that are only available to your TikTok followers.

4. Common pitfalls to avoid when monetizing on TikTok

Monetizing on TikTok can be a great way to earn money, but it's important to avoid some common pitfalls. Here are some tips to keep in mind:

Don't compromise your values: Make sure you're only partnering with brands that align with your own values and mission.

CHAPTER 7: BEST PRACTICES AND STRATEGIES FOR SUCCESS

TikTok can be a powerful tool for growing your business or personal brand, but it's important to have a solid strategy in place to ensure your success.

In this chapter, we'll explore some of the best practices and strategies for achieving success on TikTok.

1. Maintain consistency on TikTok

Consistency is key when it comes to building a following on TikTok. Here are some tips for maintaining consistency on TikTok:

Create a content calendar: Plan out your content in advance and create a schedule that you can stick to. This will help you stay organized and ensure that you're posting regularly.

Use a content theme: Consider using a specific theme for your content that aligns with your niche or brand. This will help your content stand out and make it easier for your audience to recognize your brand.

Stick to a posting schedule: Consistency is key when it comes to building a following on TikTok. Make sure you're posting regularly and at a consistent time each day to keep your audience engaged.

2. Analyze your TikTok performance and adjust your strategy

Analyzing your TikTok performance is essential for maximizing your success on the platform. Here are some tips for analyzing your performance and adjusting your strategy:

Use TikTok Analytics: TikTok offers a built-in analytics tool that provides insights into your performance. Use these insights to identify which content is performing well and adjust your strategy accordingly.

Monitor your engagement rate: Your engagement rate is a key metric that can help you identify which content is resonating with your audience. Make sure you're tracking your engagement rate and adjusting your strategy accordingly.

Experiment with new content formats: TikTok is constantly evolving, and new content formats are being introduced all the time. Experiment with new formats like live streams, duets, and challenges to see what works best for your audience.

5. **Common mistakes to avoid when using TikTok for business or personal branding**

There are some common mistakes that businesses and individuals make when using TikTok for branding or business. Here are some tips for avoiding these mistakes:

Don't use TikTok solely for self-promotion: TikTok is a social media platform, which means it's important to engage with your audience and provide value beyond just self-promotion.

Don't ignore your audience: Engage with your audience by responding to comments and direct messages. This will help build a stronger connection with your followers and increase engagement.

Don't post low-quality content: Quality is important on TikTok. Make sure you're creating high-quality content that resonates with your audience and aligns with your brand.

6. Advanced TikTok strategies for maximizing engagement and growth

For businesses and individuals who are serious about growing their presence on TikTok, there are some advanced strategies that can be used to maximize engagement and growth. Here are some tips:

Collaborate with other creators: Collaborating with other creators can help you reach a new audience and increase engagement. Look for other creators in your niche and reach out to them to see if they're interested in collaborating.

Use hashtags strategically: Hashtags are an important tool for reaching new audiences on TikTok. Make sure you're using relevant hashtags and avoid using too many in a single post.

Consider paid advertising: Paid advertising can be an effective way to reach a wider audience on TikTok. Consider running a paid ad campaign to increase your visibility and reach more people.

CHAPTER 8: CONCLUSION

Congratulations! You have made it to the end of this e-book on how to use TikTok to grow your business or personal brand. We hope that by now, you have gained valuable insights into the world of TikTok and how it can help you promote your brand and grow your following. Throughout this e-book, we have highlighted numerous benefits of using TikTok for business or personal branding. Here's a quick recap:

Reach a younger audience: TikTok has become one of the most popular social media platforms among Gen Z and millennials. By using TikTok, you can reach a younger audience and connect with them in a fun and engaging way.

Build brand awareness: TikTok's algorithm is designed to promote engaging and creative content. By creating content that resonates with your target audience, you can increase your brand awareness and attract new followers.

Showcase your products or services: TikTok is a great platform to showcase your products or services in a unique and creative way. Whether you're promoting a new product or demonstrating how your services work, TikTok can help you get your message across.

Build a community: TikTok allows you to engage with your followers on a more personal level. By responding to comments and creating content that speaks to their interests, you can build a loyal community of followers who will support your brand.

Before you start creating TikTok content, here are some final tips and recommendations to help you use TikTok successfully:

Know your audience: Understanding your target audience is essential to creating content that resonates with them. Take the time to research your audience and find out what kind of content they enjoy.

Be authentic: TikTok is all about authenticity. Don't be afraid to be yourself and show your personality in your content.

Be consistent: Consistency is key when it comes to building a following on TikTok. Try to post at least once a day to keep your followers engaged.

Use trending hashtags: Using trending hashtags can help you reach a wider audience and get your content seen by more people.

If you haven't already, I encourage you to start using TikTok to grow your business or personal brand. With its growing popularity and engaged audience, TikTok presents a unique opportunity for brands to connect with their followers and attract new ones. Remember, the key to success on TikTok is to be creative, authentic, and consistent. With these tips in mind, you'll be well on your way to building a successful TikTok presence and growing your business or personal brand. Good luck!

Download My Free Gift

Inflation Busters: Discover 10 Life-Changing Online Businesses
You Can Start Today To Boost Your Income

Visit My Website

Fidelis Reviews

 Health for Fitness